MW01234397

All scripture quotations are taken from the New International Version (NIV) of the Bible.

Edited by Hope Girard Atwell.

If you would like to contact the author you can email her at lettersfromhim@yahoo.com

Forward

"letters from Him" by Prophetess Katherine Lynn is a must read for all of those seeking to hear a word from God. Katherine Lynn takes a very different approach to the prophetic by using some of the most common of names, hearing the voice of God, and speaking into the lives of those who bear those names. Wow! I know that anyone who wants to be encouraged by God or who wants to encourage others through God's word, should get a copy of this work. You will be blessed.

Dr. Deborah Harrell Isom author of "So You Say You are a Prophet"

Introduction

We all have a gift and we all are called to do God's work. My calling is the office of a Prophet. This means that I can hear the voice of God for others.

What is Prophecy? Prophecy signifies the speaking forth of the mind and counsel of God.

Prophecy is the forth telling of the will of God whether it tells the past, present or future. (Vines Complete Expository Dictionary, p. 893)

1 Corinthians 14:3 (NIV) but everyone who prophesies speaks to men for their strengthening, encouragement and comfort.

I have received several prophesies by different prophets who have told me that I would use my gift of prophecy to bring healing and restoration to the nations. I have questioned how I would be able to do that. One day God said to me;

Katherine, I am going to start giving you names and I want you to write to them what I say. In doing this I will be able to reach a multitude of my people.

So many of my people are lost and alone, and this book will be used as a tool to reach many letting them know that, I love them, I am still here and I am listening. I want each of them to know that I will never give up on them and there is nothing they can do or have done that will change that. I want them to remember that my love is never failing and never changing.

Please know that in reading this book if you find your life story under the name of someone else take that prophecy to be your own. God's word is ever expanding it has no limits or boundaries. Remember we are all His. He does not define us by our name or actions. He sees us as complete and perfect. This is the time to come back to Him. This is the season of a new awakening in the body of Christ.

When you read this book please remember that it is important to take your letter to God for yourself. You should pray about it. Prophecy is not a quick fix to any situation it is a way of letting you know in part what God has in store for you and to help you get from where you are to where you should be. A prophecy that you get today may not come to pass for several years. On the other hand it could happen tomorrow. A prophetic word is hope for a better tomorrow by knowing that God still loves you today.

~ This book is dedicated to my children

Cameron, Nyah and Micah ~

I have been able to see who I am through the eyes of you. I thank you for showing me what true love is. I thank you for helping me grow. I thank you that you have kept me grounded, focused and inspired.

I Love You!!!!!

Table of Contents

Abigail

I see you as a little girl sitting at a round table; you are all alone. You have on a pale pink dress that has yellow daisies on it. You have one of your elbows on the table and your head is resting on it. You are pondering life and what will become of it. There seems to be sickness around you and it has you concerned. I see your father coming to comfort you which helps ease your fear and worry.

Abigail, the Lord says He has always been with you, even in the darkest hours. He says He hears your cries and He sees your tears. He says that the pain of yesterday will not always be your tomorrow; you are turning a new leaf. He knows you want to be a school teacher and you will be. He is going to fill your life with many children, ones that have struggles, and you will use all the lessons you learned as a child and be a guiding light for the little ones who are temporarily lost. He says your fear and worry will fade with each child you save. He Loves you and is very proud of you. You are now and always will be His sweet girl.

Alexandria

The Lord says your life has been like the sun that shines through the branches of a tree. He says when you walk under the branches you are mostly in the shadows and less in the sun. Most of your life you have felt like you have been in the shadows; somewhat forgotten; somewhat misunderstood. Every now and then you have felt confident enough to let your light shine but then you go back into the safety of the shadows.

Alexandria, the Lord says it is time to come out of the shadows. He says you will always be in the safety of His shadow but it is time to shine. You are ready to be all that you were created to be. He says that you have a passion for singing. You are going to be able to break strongholds off those who are still *lost in the shadow of the misunderstood. Have no fear, for He is with you. He is so proud of you; He says He loves you.*

Alyssa

The Lord says you have never been one to complain, you pretty much just go with the flow. He says you don't ask for much and are one to be happy with what you have. He says that life has not been all you would have liked for it to have been. You have a huge heart and you love giving of yourself, but sometimes you give so much you don't have enough left for you. He says that you love to serve and that is the sign of a leader. He says you want to have your own catering business and you will. It is time for you to get back all of yourself that you have given away. He says that you will be amazed when you see the blessing come in, because you never expect them to. He says that you deserve such sweetness. He never wants you to settle for anything that is not worthy of you. He has the perfect mate for you and you will know it is him when you meet him. You will experience joy you never thought was possible. He says that you are a blessing and He is excited for you. He says He loves you.

Amanda

The Lord says that you may not take your life. He says even though you feel like the water is almost above your head, and the only thing keeping you alive are your kids, a change is coming. He knows your loss and your pain. He wants to take it all away; all you have to do is give it to Him. He says to stand up, look in the mirror and see the beauty that He sees. You have so much love, compassion, grace and knowledge inside of you. He says you don't share it because you don't think anyone would want to hear from you; you are wrong. He says with the storms you have weathered, people would have no choice but to listen to you. They will say, "If she can do it I can do it too." He says to fight for yourself and He will fight with you. He says He hurts for you and He will take your tears and fill your heart

21

with the love it is meant to carry. He
says "just trust me my angel. " He says
He loves you.

Amber

The Lord says you are a very driven person. You know what you want and you go after it, and most of the time you get it. He says even though you usually get what you want there always seems to be something missing. You keep looking but no matter what you achieve you still feel like something is missing and it makes you angry. You are a very independent person and you don't like asking for help. He says that being strong comes naturally to you and you get frustrated because you don't understand why people just don't get it.

Amber, the Lord says that sometimes the drive pushing you is also the drive keeping you from what is missing. You used to have a relationship with Him but one day you decided you were better off without Him and that's the day you became so independent and that's the day something became missing. He says if you choose to come back to Him the anger, frustration, and constant searching will end. He can't wait to walk and talk with you because He misses you. He says He loves you.

Amy

When I asked the Lord what He wanted to say to you He just smiled and said "blue jeans and tennis shoes". He says you love your blue jeans and tennis shoes. You feel comfortable, like you are ready for your day. He says to get ready to come out of your blue jeans and tennis shoes; your next venture will require you to be in front of people. He says you always have liked to be in the background just blending in but you have watched from the sideline long enough. He says it is time for a promotion. He knows you didn't ask for one, you just say what will you have me do today Lord and you do whatever He ask. He wants you to teach teenage girls how to be servants, so many have forgotten how to serve, most just want to lead. He says for this task you are the perfect servant to lead. He says when

you show up He will lead you to victory.
He is so thankful for your submissive
spirit. He says He loves you.

Angela

The Lord showed me a yard full of bird houses. He said you love bird houses. He said you love the beauty that birds possess; you love the colors and the awe of the birds. He said you find yourself getting lost in their splendor and you use them as a distraction from yourself. When you look in the mirror you can't see the beauty and splender within yourself so you live through the birds.

Angela, the Lord said, my beautiful hummingbird you are the most beautiful of all. The reflection in the mirror is only a glimpse of the splendor that you possess. You are a treasure. As much joy as you get from watching the birds is as much joy as He gets from watching you. You possess a beauty that only comes from true purity. You *are so special. Your inner beauty is going to captivate the outer flesh and you are going to be the one others cling to. You are going to be able to reach down into the inner most being of the unloved and fill them with compassion and beauty that only comes from within. You will be what others can't and you will be able to speak life into areas that were thought to be dead. Don't worry my little hummingbird, your time is coming and your beauty will never fade. He says He loves you.*

Anna

I see you in a big room you have on a pink dress with frilly lace. You are dancing in circles laughing, playing and dreaming of one day being a ballerina. There is nothing that brings you more joy than you and the dance.

I see you as a young lady; you are hanging up your dress and leotard, you are sad and have a heavy burden. It seems that a darkness has fallen and you have lost the love you once had for the dance. Something has come and stolen the one thing that could change any rainy day into your rainbow. Life has now become a stranger to you and you no longer want to participate. It's like the light that once shone so brightly has been snuffed out.

Anna, the Lord says that He knows the pain and hurt that you are feeling. He feels the loneliness inside your heart. He wants you to know that change is coming and you are going to be a dancer again. He is going to bring life back into your feet. He knows that you want to spin again. He says, take my hand my daughter and we will dance together. He will show you things about yourself that you don't even remember. The change you have been praying for is coming, don't give up. Stand up, take His hand and get ready for the dance that will last a life time. He says He loves you.

Autumn

The Lord says that through life you have felt like no one takes you seriously. You get very upset because you try so hard but still you remain just a kid. Even with age you are still treated as if you were a child. He says not to worry; He has not given you a child-like heart to help those whose heart has become hard. Your fun-loving personality will help them remember what life was like before they became so hard-hearted and being a child at heart is not a curse, it is a calling. The ones who used to not take you seriously will. He only gives a child-like heart to the most mature. What He gives is not a mistake, trust Him. You will understand and the more you show others, the more you will understand. He says to love life as only you can and be an example to those who *have forgotten how. He says He loves you.*

Beth

The Lord wants you to know that you are not overlooked. He knows that it seems that you stand in the shadows a lot. He has placed you there on purpose because, just as the verse says in Psalm 91, he who dwells in the shelter of the Most High will rest in the shadows of the Almighty. He says that you are that shelter, you are the resting place. The lost and broken seem to be drawn to you because you are the shadow of the Almighty. You are walking in your purpose and you are not forgotten, you are called. He will continue to send the broken and lost to you as long as you are waiting in His shadow. He says He loves you.

Bethany

The Lord says that you are a seeker and that you love to find the good in all people. You never look for the bad and are surprised when it shows up. Even when you see the bad, you still look for the good. You have a compassionate heart that enjoys the beauty of the world; even the smallest of things bring you joy. People are drawn to you because of your kind spirit. You love all people for their potential, not their present. He says that you have come to a pause in your potential; you have hit a wall and are stuck. He says that you just feel tired and need a pause. Don't give up on you. This is not as good as it gets. Your present is not even close to your potential; you have so much more to offer the world. He says the gift you possess can be tiring but if you give your burdens to Him, He will carry *them so, you can continue to bring goodness out of the present. He says that He loves you.*

Beverly

The Lord says that you find yourself questioning why no one listens to you. You are an extremely intelligent person who holds a vast amount of knowledge but still it seems that no one will listen. The Lord says that there is a difference between listening and hearing. He says people hear you, they just choose not to listen. The knowledge you offer does not fall on fallow ground. He says that when you speak you plant a seed and even though you don't see the fruit that does not mean it's not there. He says keep planting the seeds and the fruit will come. He says they may not listen but they hear. He says He loves you.

Cameron

The Lord wants to know why you are running? He says there is no amount of distance you can put between you and Him. You are a very special creation, and are here for many purposes. He says that the easy way out will never work for you. You are called to greatness but that thought you can't comprehend. You are stuck in the reality of research that you have stored in your mind. He says that no matter how much you try to not face it, you know it is true. The proof has already been seen, it's just the grasping you are struggling with. Once you have accepted who you really are, instead of who you want to be things will be a lot simpler for you, because you won't be walking into the wind; the wind will be walking with you. He says your calling is beyond your mistakes. Your mistakes *are because you are not ready for your calling. Your desire to help others has gotten lost and is being used in the wrong way. Right now, you are lost in the haze of the exciting unknown but soon, you will be ready to embrace the call that has been placed on your life. The light that the enemy has stolen to shine darkness will be turned around and you will begin to start walking in the truth of who you are. Once you see the fruit of you, and all you are called to be, the more you will walk with the wind. He says He loves you.*

Candace

The Lord showed me a picture of a vase. It was so beautiful. I have never seen a vase so beautiful. Then I heard the sound you would hear if someone blew over the top of an empty bottle. The Lord says that they are both you. You are so beautiful but so empty. All of your life you been told how beautiful you are, but words are all you ever heard. He says that it is the actions that have left you so empty. You have tried to fill your vase with the things you thought would fill the emptiness but nothing seemed to work. The more you put in the emptier you became and this has gone on for many years. You have been empty for so long, you don't care how long the happiness lasts, or how much you have to endure to keep it, it's better than being so empty.

Candace, the Lord says that you and He have had a few moments together and every now and then you let Him in but then you shut Him out again. He says if you just trust Him, He will fill you with everlasting joy. He wants to take the emptiness from you and fill you with the things you deserve and long for. He says you are worth more than you can imagine. You have so many promises waiting for you and once you get full, you will have an amazing testimony that will change the lives of many men and women. He says that your level of compassion exceeds your momentary emptiness. He says He is waiting for you. He says He loves you.

Caroline

The Lord showed me a little girl in a room with a bunch of doors and she keeps going in circles because she doesn't know which door to go through. This little girl is very insecure and lonely. She has not had much love and proper attention. She is afraid to choose a door because if she chooses the wrong one she may get lost again and end up back in the room of doors.

Caroline, the Lord says He is going to show you the right door to go through. He says all you have to do is walk through it and trust that He will be with you when you enter. On the other side of the door you will experience real love, affirmation, attention, joy, peace and praise. He knows that you are tired and He wants to take it all away. Give Him all your cares and worries and He will trade them for peace and gladness. He doesn't want you to be lonely and afraid anymore. He wants to spend time with you and walk with you through the door to your healing and victory. He says He loves you.

Casey

The Lord gave me the word hope. He said that for a long time you were walking lost in a haze of confusion. No matter where you have looked, there has been nothing but fog and darkness. One morning you woke up, and without knowing why you walked into a church. You sat and listened to the choir singing and before you knew it you were at the altar. He says that when you stood up you could see clearly for the first time in ten years. He says that you have not cried like that in a long time. It was like you released a river of regret and sadness. You were washed clean that day and since then, you have walked in the light. He says that you have not strayed from the path that He has laid for you. You have become the light of hope for many that are lost in the dark. He wants you to start a support group at your church for the women who are trapped in the dark fog. He says that they will trust you and your testimony will allow them release from the river they are aimlessly drifting on. He says then He will fill them with the river of flowing waters that will allow them to walk in the light for others to see. He says that He believes in you. He says He loves you.

Cassandra

What a huge heart you have! The Lord says it has not always been so easy to give yourself away the way you do. For a long time you kept your heart, mind, body, and emotions guarded. Life taught you that if you let someone in they would hurt you. He says that you lost more than you ever gained. He says that family was not an easy thing to have and you had to fight to even be able to say the word family. He says that you had a hard childhood and for a while, you had to be the parent; you had to grow up way to fast.

Cassandra, the Lord says the woman you are now is the woman you were created to be. You fought hard and gave a lot of pain to Him and, because of that, you are now able to give yourself away to others, you are now able to help others. He says that you have a heart for the hurting and unloved. He says that you do not like to see anyone alone or feeling lonely. You are able to love those who others have forgotten. He says that you will do even greater things. You will begin to be put in places where you will be able to teach others the wonders of true love. Most think true love comes in only one form but you will be able to show them true loves comes in many shapes, sizes and colors. He says that true love comes from the one true heart and that is His. You will be able to teach others that love has no boundaries it is for everyone to feel and share. He says that He loves you.

Chelsea

The Lord says you are an amazingly good person. He says you do not hear that enough. You have been surrounded by negative and hurtful situations as long as you can remember and you have endured them all. He says you have been strong even when you felt so weak. He says that you are a wonderful mother whose children absolutely adore you.

Chelsea, the Lord says He is going to replace the entire negative for positive and the hurt with happiness. You will no longer have to worry about the future for your children because they are going to be blessed by watching you come through the storm. He says that you are raising up mighty warriors who will make you proud. He says He is going to finish the journey with you.

He is proud of you for never giving up.
He says He loves you.

Cheryl

The Lord says sometimes you get caught between two mindsets. He says that life has been so hard you have created a way of escaping. You get so lost in the carefree world that sometimes you can't find your way back. You even get so caught up in the lives of others it seems like their lives and problems become yours and then you have to go back into your lost mindset to escape the pain you just claimed.

Cheryl, the Lord says He wants you to be still and rest. He says you are so tired from running and being lost that you physically hurt. Your body is breaking down from all the journeys that you take. He knows that you love helping others, but for a season, He wants you to focus on you. You have pressed your life so far down you can't even remember why you are always in pain.   You will get to the point of walking in your gifting but for now He wants to just love on you. He says that you are an amazing person who loves deeply. He says that you will be whole, healed and set free. He just wants to spend some time with you. He says He loves you.

Chloe

I see you dancing with ribbons. You are standing still but your arms are moving the ribbons; it's like you are painting the air. You are so graceful when you move the ribbons, it looks so effortless. Your eyes are closed and it seems you are not even breathing. The Lord says you are in a battle. He says that you are painting the lines of defense. He says you are an intercessor and this is your way of praying for the ones He puts on your heart. He says you stand tall and wave your banner until the battle is over. He says not many go to battle this way but He wants you to start teaching your battle cry to others. He wants you to show others that it's okay to be creative when in battle. He says the color of your tears and love is beautiful. He says that you create an armor of many colors. He says he loves you.

Christie

The Lord gave me the phrase "courage under fire". He says that you can't see it but that's who you are. He says that's why so much happens in your life, because you are courage under fire. When you grasp this truth, you will no longer run; you will face all that life throws at you with courage. He says you seem to withdraw and hide a lot because you have not found the courage that lives within you. He says that you find it in the love of others. He said that protection and security are everything to you because that is your gifting. He says that you are the restorer of the places that others have broken into and violated. He says that young girls will come to you for refuge, protection and security. You will be able to teach them how to find the courage they need to face the brokenness inside of them so they can feel safe again. He knows you are scared, but He will be with you. He says you won't be alone, He will send others to stand with you while you are being courageous under fire. He says He loves you.

Clara

The Lord says you have just begun to walk in your calling. He says you are to raise up the children. He is going to place you in what others would call unchangeable situations. He says you will be with the children others would walk away from and you will be able to relate to them. You will be able to speak in a way that they understand. He says you have the ability to adapt to any situation and bring peace. You are an amazing teacher who loves deeply. Your life has not always been easy but you have persevered. The lessons life has taught, you will teach to others. While teaching the children, you will show them they are valuable and worthy. He says you truly believe that no child will be left behind. He says time has no end when it comes to the love of a child and you will love unconditionally and openly. He says that you will build up the next generation to be strong warriors who know who He is. He says He is so proud of you. He says that He loves you.

Darlene

The Lord says that you have come through so much; you have traveled so far. He says you have walked through fire to the point where you don't think you can take another step. He says you have such a determined character and you refuse to see defeat. He says that you stand tall.

Darlene, the Lord says He wants you to rest in Him for a while but you don't remember how to rest. He says He wants you to learn how to just be Darlene again. You have begun to believe the best way to get through the fire is to put yourself second and take care of someone else. The Lord says that having a caring, helping heart is a beautiful thing but He wants you to take care of yourself. He wants to love on you. He says He wants to walk with you through your fire. He wants you to be able to look those you are helping in the eyes with no shame and no fear and allow them to see the brokenness inside you. You have the most loving heart and will bless many. You possess so much love and you are a kind, giving soul. He wants you at your best; so come and rest in Him, He will refresh you so that you will be able to have the confidence that you desire. He says you will do amazing things. He says He loves you.

Debra

The Lord says you are true beauty but you have not heard that in a long time. He says that you have only heard the opposite. You have been verbally abused so much you have learned to expect it and are numb to it; at least that's what you tell your heart to believe. The truth of the lie is slowly breaking every fiber of you and destroying the evidence of the true beauty that resides inside of you.

Debra, the Lord says, if you let him, He will show you who you were created to be. He says that if you allow Him to restore the broken pieces of your heart He will rebuild it and all the lies spoken over you will be just a memory of what used to be. The beauty that is hidden inside you will be exposed for all to see. When He has finished healing the emotions that have been trampled you will see how captivating you truly are. You will have a confidence the strongest of words will not be able to shake. He says you will be so strong you will be the restorer and rebuilder of the broken. He says walk with Him and be all that He created you to be. He says He loves you.

Denise

I heard the Lord say you are a mother to many but you are a daughter to none. He said you grew up alone without knowing your parents; you never knew the love of a mother or the security of a father. He said that you have walked through life alone. Even through that you seemed to know you were never truly alone. He said you found yourself in church often listening intently to the preacher, holding onto every word and every promise. He said that with every breath you grew stronger and closer to Him. He said you began to visit orphanages. He said before long you were working full time with those who, like you, walked alone. You are able to give them the love of a mother and, while doing that, you are able to teach them the security of the one true Father. He will send you to the nations to teach all that you know. Coming into the world you were alone and unloved but now you are loved more than most and will never be able to remember what being alone felt like. The lessons you will teach will be the ones that others will teach. Your students will become the most grateful of all because what you are teaching them is that they are not unlovable and never alone. He says that He is proud of you. He says He loves you.

Diana

I see you standing in the middle of a canvas, there are so many colors around you. You seem to have a lost look on your face. You are turning in circles trying to find the right color but you are afraid the one you pick might be the wrong one.

The Lord says you have allowed so many people to paint your path that you don't even know which one to take. It is time to take back the paintbrush of your life and allow Him to show you your true color. He says to think back to when you were a little girl, to when you spent hours painting & coloring, spending time just laughing and talking to Him. You will be able to remember all the things you talked about with Him. He says your favorite color is blue. You love to sit and stare at the sky and watch the clouds during the day and the sunset at night you loved the way the sun looked like it was going into the water. He says not to worry, those happy feelings are going to come back; He is going to restore all that life has taken from you. He says He is going to change the ashes to beauty. You are going to be set free from feeling captive to your past. You are going to be so full of life that you are going to want to share your testimony with everyone. He sees you having an art studio on the ocean front and in that studio you are going to counsel the ones who are lost in a sea of colors. He says you are going to help them remember their favorite color. He says He loves everything about you. He says you are beautiful shade of blue.

Diane

I see you standing in a greenhouse surrounded by many beautiful plants. You seem to have an amazing love for nature and all the beauty it provides. The Lord says that you have spent many hours studying all the different types of plants and have chosen the most unique and rarest to be in your greenhouse. He says you love the challenge and the sense of accomplishment. He says you love what comes from the smallest of seeds. He says when you step out of the greenhouse you disappear, you become the smallest of seeds. You feel that you are waiting on something and you don't know what it is so you feel lost and alone. That's why you love plants so much, because you know that with the right amount of dirt, water, and love the seed will grow into a beautiful plant bringing happiness to anyone who sees it. He says that your time is coming and that He will provide all you need. He will provide the soil, the nourishment, the water, and the love that you my little seed will begin to grow. You will be rooted in Him and will have so many blossoms that you will bless many women. Your heart's desire is to bring joy to the hearts of women and you will do that. He says get ready to grow and spread His love. He says He loves you.

Donna

The Lord says, "Remember when you were a little girl and you thought the world was a grand place? You had the biggest imagination. Remember when you used to day dream about who you would become; what you would look like, who you would marry and what your job would be? Wasn't that awesome?"

Donna, the Lord says He is sorry things did not turn out the way you imagined. Life happened so fast for you and now you just sit and wonder what went wrong? Where did the time go? What happened to my dreams? How did this become my life? He says your biggest question is what did I do to deserve this life?

Donna, the Lord says you don't deserve the life you are living. He says that it will get better. You are going to find the courage you need to step out in faith; knowing that, if you step out, things will change. He says when you step out, you will find there is a whole world out there and in that you will find the help and support you need to stay strong. In your strength you will begin to pray and forgive those who have hurt you and in that forgiveness you will forgive yourself. He says that is where the real healing will come from. He says you have so much to offer. You love to see the good in people. He says that you have come through so much. Do not doubt the outcome but instead, embrace the moment by moment change. He will be with you to help take the pain as you give it to Him. He says that you are so much stronger than you think. Trust Him and He will be by your side. He says that He loves you.

Duchess

The Lord says that he hears your cries. He knows that you wonder why they named you Duchess when there is nothing royal about you or your life. He knows the hurt and pain that life has caused you and He knows that you wonder why you are even here.

Duchess, the Lord says that you are royalty, you have been set apart and you are a prized jewel. He says life has happened to you in many hurtful ways but you never gave up. You have gotten lost, confused, trampled on and have lived in the dark for a long time but you never gave up. You have sacrificed so much but it is time for a change. He says to get ready because the seeds you have planted are getting ready to bloom. You've never stopped believing, trusting and having faith that if you held on for one more day everything would be ok. He says today is the day! He says the harvest is ready and your fruit is ripe. You are a beautiful gardener who plants the sweetest of seeds. The seeds you plant can only be planted by royalty. He says, "Well done my good and faithful servant." He says He loves you.

Elaine

The Lord says for a long time you felt like you had to be the glue that held all the pieces of the puzzle called your life together. He says that over the years this has really weighed you down. It seems the more you give the more they take and the more they take, the more you break. He says you fear if you move it will all fall. He says, "Elaine my dear, it is okay if it falls. They can't move until you do. How can they ever depend on Me if you keep them together? It is okay to let them fall. You have seasoned the ground it is not a fallow land. If they fall, they will be planted. I will water them and they will grow. The more you let go, the more freedom you will have to do the things I have called you to do. You are to be the support of the lost girls. You are strong enough to glue them back together, plow the ground ahead of them, place them in their rows and let them grow. You have learned over the years all you'll need for the task set before you. All you have to do is release the ones that have you glued to the puzzle that you are holding together. He says He loves you."

Elizabeth

The Lord says that you have always been so full of life. You have always known what you wanted and didn't want out of life. Life has surprised you from time to time and you've had your share of struggles. Disappointment was just a reason to try harder and giving up is not an option for you. He says you are an encourager and you love deeply. You don't like to see sadness. You love your family with every fiber of your being. He says that your heart's desire is to help the lost. You are a wonderful teacher. He is so proud of you. You will lead many to the kingdom. He says you are just beginning to see the wonders He has in store for you; you are just getting started. He says to never settle. You will achieve greatness because you will take many with you on your journey. He says He loves you.

Emily

The Lord says that your life has been like the Wizard of Oz. He says that sometimes you don't know if you are asleep or awake. You wish it were all a dream and that you could wake up and all the storms would be gone. He says that your life has been a series of tornadoes and you never know when they are coming. You are to the point where you hate when everything is still, sunny and calm because that usually means the next one is about to hit. You never have time to clean up the mess from the first one before the next one comes. The people in your life really don't want to help and if anything, they seem to scatter until the storm is over.

Emily, the Lord says you have been considering going to church. He says you are afraid because you don't know anyone there and you have become comfortable and are accustomed to the chaos. Don't be afraid, the church He has put on your heart to visit is the perfect fit for you. He says that they will help you through the storms and help bring calm and order to your life so that you can get the help and healing you need. Once you get the calm you need you will become a storm chaser for those who are lost in their own storm. He says you will be surprised at how good you will be at calming storms instead of just enduring them. The best part of all is that you will be proud of yourself for all you have accomplished. He says you have not felt that in a long time. He is excited to take this journey with you. He says He loves you.

Erica

The Lord showed me a picture of a rose. He says ever since you were a little girl you couldn't wait to blossom. You have always wanted to be loved and adored. He says that you loved dressing like a princess and dreaming of the day that your prince would come. You knew exactly what your wedding would look like and you had it all planned out. Now that you are older, your view of your prince has changed. There has been some heartache and heartbreak that has made your view not as much like a fairytale anymore. He says that you are not even sure if you believe in love, trust, security or family.

Erica, the Lord says all that you saw when you were a little girl was through the eyes of purity and the heart of innocence. He says that He wants to take you back there. Your prince is still going to come. You need to prepare your heart for him. The path that you are on is not the path He created for you. You tell yourself all the time, when you are looking in the mirror, "Today I will be stronger. Today I will make a change." When you walk away from the mirror, the fear and distraction return. He says He wants to help you get back onto the right path. You are stronger than you think. All it takes is that first step then they will get easier and easier. There are a lot of children out there waiting on you. He says that you have such a love for the kids. Once you get back on the right path, you will help a multitude of little ones who just need a loving hug or warm smile that only you can give. He says that you are getting ready to become the blossom of the most beautiful and fragrant rose of all. He says He loves you.

Erin

The Lord says that being the middle child is never easy. You are neither the first nor the last so you end up feeling lost and forgotten, but you are neither. He says you are in the middle for a reason. He wants you to see that, sometimes, being in the middle is what holds things together. You have the ability to keep things calm. He has called you to be voice of reason. You enjoy helping others through hard and rough situations. You are like a counselor, even though you have no formal training; life has been your educator. He will use you to be the calm that holds the storm still long enough for others to see what caused the storm and what changes need to be made to calm the storm. You will be the best storm chaser because you won't even have to look for them, they will come to you. You will bring understanding and peace just by being you. He says He loves you.

Evelyn

The Lord says that He missed you at church today. He knows that between work, kids, your marriage and everything that life is throwing at you, you are surprised that you are still standing. He says to remember that you are never standing alone, He will never leave you.

Evelyn, the Lord says that when you are worshiping Him He loves it. You go so deep into the spirit you forget where you are. He loves when you come into the throne room and sit on His lap. He loves your smile and laughter. He wants you to know that He has your children in the palm of His hand. He says to give them to Him and trust that He will take care of them. It's okay if they fall; you have given them a good foundation and road map. Even if they stumble or lose their way they will not get lost because of all you have taught them. He says for your marriage, keep praying for him, he will come around. Don't give up on him. He says your husband is sad and afraid but He says that He is working on his heart. The Lord says you have shown Him that you are faithful with giving when you have little to give, so He is going to trust you with much. A change in your finances is coming; a promotion that you have been praying for is about to happen. He says to get ready for abundance. The Lord says you are about to step out into ministry and when that happens; those around you will be moved because you did not let life defeat you. In the midst of all the turmoil you chose to praise Him and in doing that you will encourage others to do the same. He says do not let fear stand in the way of all your potential. He says that are a natural born fighter.

You will achieve all you put your mind to. He will forever be in your corner. He says He loves you.

Glenda

The Lord says that you are stronger than you think. He says you have endured more than most. Each time you fall you get up, dust yourself off and keep walking. He says that when the tears flow, you know you have begun to heal and when the singing starts, you are facing the pain. You have the ability to let things go quickly; this is a gift. Even though you are gifted does not mean you don't feel pain. He says that you are a burden bearer so you feel the pain of others. He is going to start sending people to you that do not know how to dust themselves off. You will be able to teach them how to walk, cry and sing their way into a brighter today; you will show them hope. They live in a dark yesterday but with you helping them, they will worship in a brilliant tomorrow. He says He loves you.

Gloria

I see you playing a violin. You have your eyes closed and you are lost in the music, it is like you and the violin are one. I see tears flowing down your face. You are not crying for yourself, you are crying for the ones you love. The Lord says that when you play your violin it is like you are going to battle for the ones you love who are lost or hurting and the violin is your weapon. He hears your heart and has counted and saved all the tears you have cried. He is getting ready to return all the tears. He will begin to pour your tears over the ones you cry for and they will start to feel refreshed and renewed, those who are sick will become well and those who are lost will be washed clean. You are an amazing weapon of warfare. He loves the way you love with the love of Christ. He is so thankful for you. He says that you have stored up many treasures in heaven. He says that you are going too blessed in the morning and blessed in the evening. He is proud of you and He loves you.

Grace

The Lord says that beauty is not an option for you. He says that beauty to most is a blessing but to you, at times it, is a curse. You sometimes wish for the beauty to go away. You wish to make it through the day without someone giving you the pleasing smile, the adored wink or the perfect compliment. He says that you have heard these all of your life. Even as a child, you felt you were on display for the entire world to see. Over time, all you came to be was a beautiful shell. The Lord says your beauty will never fail but that which lies beneath the shell will manifest itself. Your desire is for people to see the real you who is even more beautiful underneath the shell. He is going to put you in places where your outer beauty will allow you to go so that your inner beauty will prevail. The ones who really need you will see the real you and that is where you will come alive and shine. You will be able to changes lives and speak to a multitude of people. Your beautiful shell will captivate them but your inner beauty will motivate them and give them the confidence needed to move forward. He says your gentle spirit will allow them to trust you and in trusting they will learn to trust Him. He says you and He together will love the hate out of the unloved. He says to stay beautiful. He loves the way you love Him. He says He loves you.

Gretchen

The Lord says that your season of study is over and it is time to go from the student to the teacher. He knows that you love to sit and observe. He says you are getting ready to move into leadership. You are full of much wisdom and knowledge. You have the ability to sweetly speak truth into any situation. When you speak, even though you speak with a sweet voice, it is full of wisdom. Your voice demands any chaos to come to order. When you speak it is as if all things stand still. He says that your timing is perfect. He says that you have the ability to apply all your knowledge in any situation. You are quick to listen and slow to speak. You really don't think your words hold much value or that anyone would want to hear what you have to say, that is far from the truth. He says that because you speak with such wisdom people will listen. He wants you to start speaking life into people's lives. Continue to follow His lead and you will be a bright light for the dark at heart to see. He says that you are His little light. He says He loves you.

Gwendolyn

The Lord says you have always been the voice of reason, the wise one. He says that sometimes you say, "Who will be wise for me?" Sometimes you get so tired but you tuck it away in case someone needs you to be strong. He says it's okay not to be strong today. He is, and always will be, your strength and voice of reason. He says that's why you have stayed so strong for so long, you completely rely on Him for everything. Sometimes you push yourself beyond where you should be pushed and that's why you get so tired. Now is the time to expand your boundaries. You have trained many strong young voices of reason. It's time to release some of the burdens of today onto the ones of tomorrow. He says you have taught them well, and it's time to allow them to walk it out. This is your season to see the fruit of your labor blossom into beautiful works of art. He says you are to let the wisdom flow from you as you set them free to be all that you and He has trained them to be. He says to not worry, you will still be needed and they will still come to you for answers and you will still come to Him with the questions. He says you will just be sitting in a new seat. Handing over the position is a promotion. He says it is not over, it's a new beginning. Embrace and enjoy your new promotion, you have earned it. He is very proud of you. He says He loves you.

Hallie

The Lord took me to Psalms 92 which is a song for the Sabbath day. He says you have an angelic voice. He says that when you sing, all of heaven stops to listen. He says you sing from your spirit and not your mind. You have been having a hard time wanting to sing lately, your spirit has been crushed and the passion that once burned inside is no longer there.

Hallie, the Lord has a request of you. He says that during your prayer time, when it is just you and Him, He wants you to pray in song. He wants you to release your pain and hurt to Him in song. If you see that you can sing, even during the pain, you will see that your passion is still there, it's just hidden. He says what He has joined together no man can separate and He united you

91

with song before you were placed on this earth. He says never let any person steal what was given by Him. He says that your gift is too precious to be hidden by anything. He wants you to sing through the pain and praise Him in the victory. He says He loves you.

Hannah

I see you at a crossroad and it seems as if you have been there for a while but you just can't seem to decide which way to go. The Lord says you have been at this crossroad before. He says that you never choose, you just turn back around. No one has ever given you the confidence you need, no one has ever praised you or lifted you up or taught you how to stand tall. He says that when it comes to the crossroad, fear of failure sets in and you turn around to go back to the familiar. He says that you have said that it's easier to stick to the known; at least there you know what to expect.

Hannah, the Lord says that all you have to do is just keep walking when you get to the crossroads; don't look to the left or right. He says that you will be amazed by what's on the other side. All that you could imagine or hope for is on the other side. He is there waiting for you. He wants to fill you with peace, joy love and laughter. He says that you deserve so much because you give so much of yourself. He says that even when you don't have anything left to give you give your time. He is going to bless you with abundance and the joy you have been praying for is coming. He says that your blessing is coming. He will meet you at the crossroads and He will help you walk across. He says to take His hand, have faith and He will carry you. He says He loves you.

Heather

What a childhood you had! The Lord says you have always been able to find the silver lining in any situation. He says family has always been important to you. You have made a lot of sacrifices and have had more than your share of heartache and let downs but you seem to be able to get up, dust yourself, and those who fell with you, off and keep moving. You were able to encourage those around you who were not as strong as you. You love deeply and true. Your heart is golden and when you offer your heart, it's genuine, and a better friend one can't find. He says that you are on a course for greatness. Many will try to distract you but you will always follow the voice of reason. He says that you are a blessing to everyone who knows you. The Lord says that right now, you are facing a few choices but are not sure which to choose. He says you will be able to do both. He says that family will always come first and they will support you on the path you take. Stay true to who you are, continue to trust Him and you will go far. He says that you have a love for older women and you are going to be making quilts for them. In doing that you will be restoring lost and broken families because of the love you will be pouring out. He says He loves you.

Hope

I see you standing inside of a snow globe. The Lord says that for a long time that is what your life was like. It was like you were there but not included. He says you would try to be heard but no one would listen, you were just there to be seen and, every now and then, be shaken. He says you were placed where you were needed to be seen in each moment but that was it. The day came when you broke out of the snow globe and stood on your own two feet. You fought hard to find your place outside the snow globe and now you are out and have a family. You make sure your children never feel that way; you make sure they know their words hold value. He says that is your call in life, being heard is what you teach. You will allow others to express themselves in their own language and you will make sure to let them know you heard them. He says that a silent world is not a beautiful world and He is proud of you for the words you speak. He says He loves you.

Irene

The Lord says you have spent a lot of your time looking for answers at the end of someone else's rope. He says you have thought that if you could help enough people then maybe, while doing so, you could find the answers for your own life. He says you will never find them that way.

Irene, the Lord wants you to know that you have done nothing wrong. He says you are perfect, loving, kind, considerate and compassionate. You can't change others but, if you stay true to yourself, they will choose to change themselves. He says that you sometimes give too much of yourself. He wants you to start enjoying life through your heart and not your mind. Your mind will be healed through the eyes of your heart. Let go of the things that you hold on to so tightly and see what He can do with them. He says it's okay to choose you. Give your burdens to Him and He will carry them. He knows that you love and trust Him and He wants you to enjoy your life. If you release all to Him, then life will look different and your mind will catch up with your heart. He says He loves you.

Isabella

I see you sitting on the porch. You are looking out and you see a light shining through the limbs of a tree. You are wondering what it is but you don't get up to see you go back inside. Night after night you come out to see the light and it is always there, but you never go to see what it is. The Lord says you have been taught to be afraid of the unknown and that it is better to live in the familiar darkness than to seek out the light of possibility. The Lord says He is the light that is behind the limb of the tree. He waits for you every night and He will continue to wait for you. When you are ready to talk to Him, He will be there. He says He know your fear. He wants to take that all away. He wants to be the light that lives inside of you. He wants to take away all the darkness and fear of the unknown. He wants to fill you with all the possibilities that are waiting for you. When you decide to come to Him, He will make you light for the others who are trapped in the darkness of the familiar. He says that you are a special gift and He will wait for you. He says He loves you.

Jacquelyn

I see you on a staircase. You are climbing and climbing and climbing like the stairs just keep going on forever. No matter how many steps you take you either stay at the same place or go down a little. The Lord says don't give up, my dear the burdens of yesterday will not always be so heavy. If you give Him the care and worries that you have been carrying since childhood, the stairs will be easier to climb. He knows that you have begun to accept things as they are and you have begun to find comfort in the familiar surrounds. He says that this is not where you belong. You are getting ready to come out of your comfort zone into your victory land. The days ahead will be bright and cheerful. You have not had many cheerleaders on the sidelines but He says that is about to change. You are so worried that you will pass the burdens on to your children but he says not to fear. He says that stops here and now. He says to lay them at His feet and He will carry them for you. You are about to enter into a new area of life where you will be the cheerleader for those who are stuck in familiar places. You will be able to move them and break the chains that bind them to the stairs they can't climb. He says that you will give them the courage they need to lay their burdens down. He says that you will become the coach of a mighty team. Trust Him; He has never left your side. He says He loves and adores you.

Janice

The Lord wants to know what you are looking for. He says you have spent many years looking for something. He says that you are looking for you. He says you have looked for you in different jobs, you have looked for you through the eyes of different people, you have looked for you through love and you have looked for you in the heart of your children. He says no matter where you look you can't find you.

Janice, the Lord says that you are in the palm of His hand. You reside in the beat of His heart. You are the reflection of Him. He says that you will never find you any place else. He wants you to close your eyes and remember the first time you felt His presence to the point you were in tears. He says wherever He is so are you. He says that you are everywhere because you have planted so many seeds. He says that you are a protector and you are keeping His sheep safe. He says to keep looking at your heart and you will never be lost again. He is in your heart and you are in His. He says He loves you.

Jennifer

I see you sitting on the bank of a lake. You are fishing. It's not that you care if you catch anything; it's the stillness of the water that you are fishing for. The Lord says that you have so much going on inside you, you can't even think. Sometimes it's like there are 12 people living in your head and you don't know which one to listen to so you go to the lake where it is still and quiet. As long as you are focused on the water there is peace and quiet.

Jennifer, the Lord says the reason you have so many voices in your head is because you feel like you try to talk to people but no one listens. He says that no matter how many ways you try to explain what is going on in your life no one can hear you so you just keep it all inside. The Lord says it is time to let it out. Tell Him all of your pain, sorrow, lowliness, hurt, abandonment, confusion, sickness, heartbreak, anger, emptiness, shame and bitterness He will listen. He will take it from you. He wants to trade the negative for positive. He wants to see you smile from your heart. He wants you to be as full of life as you were when you were a little girl. He just wants you to talk to Him. He wants to spend time with you. You are worth more than gold and are more precious than rubies. He says that you are truly unique and you have always known that. Others have confused your uniqueness for something else, but it is time to come back to the heart of what is truth and that truth lies in your heart. The truth is in Him. He says He loves you.

Jessica

I see you sitting on the beach. It is sunset, the colors are breath taking and you are pushing your toes deep into the cool sand. There seems to be no one on the beach but you. You are staring out at the water watching the sun go down; it looks as if you have no cares in the world. The Lord says that is far from the truth. You want people to think that you are carefree. You feel everyone expects you to be the strong one. You know exactly when to go to your favorite spot because you know that no one will be there and that's the only time you don't have to be strong. You just sit there, dig your toes in and breathe. He hears your heart. He says just as He sat the sun that night He is going to remove all the burdens from you. You have been crying out, "How long Lord, how long do I have to be strong?" He says not much longer my dear.

Jessica, He is going to send people into your life that you can trust and when they come you will know they are from Him. He knows because of your past you have a hard time trusting and the ones He sends will help tear down those strong holds that have taken over you. They will help you see the sunset and all the beautiful colors, because as many times as you have sat on the beach you have never noticed the colors. He says the scales that are covering your eyes will be removed and you will begin to feel a refreshing and light heartedness. You will begin to run again, your energy will be restored. You will even want to teach exercise classes again. He says you are going to be a refreshing spring that flows into the heart of many. You are a kind, sweet, loving and compassionate butterfly and He loves you.

Joan

I see you standing outside in the rain. It is not your typical rain, it is very colorful. I hear the Lord say that you always look for the beauty in life. He says that you don't just like the black and white. You love color and the life that it brings to any gray area. You have life in your hands. Whether it is drawing, laying on of hands to pray or just a hug, He says you bring forth life but you can't see that about yourself. He says that you will. He says that no one ever colored you. You've walked through a very gray life where there was never any beauty, just a lot of gray areas. It is hard for you to even begin to think that you are a colorful person.

Joan, the Lord says that He is going to pull the veil from your eyes and give you a new look on life. He is going to pour the beautiful colors back into you so you can begin to walk in the path created for you. The tapestry of Joan is getting ready to be completed and all will see the beauty and color in you. He says to get ready to embrace all the color of the rain. He says He loves you.

Johanna

The Lord showed me a picture of you as a little girl walking in your dad's shoes. You always wondered if you would ever be big enough to fill his shoes. All through your life it has been as if the shoes you're wearing were too big. He says you never seem to be big enough to carry all that's asked of you. It's as if you were asked to grow up and put on your big girl shoes too early and you have always felt like you failed. It is not your fault the burdens put upon you were too much to carry. He says that most grown-ups couldn't carry all that was asked of you. He says due to the feeling of failure you stopped trying as hard. You almost forgot what made you happy. You turned to things that were false to find temporary happiness so you could feel something. The happiness never really lasted and sometimes you cry out, wondering how much more you'll have to take.

Johanna, the Lord wants to take all the pain from you. He has a new pair of shoes for you, ones that are not too big, ones that will not make you feel like a failure. If you would take the leap of faith and turn to Him for happiness, you will find it will not be temporary and the need to feel will no longer be a need. He wants to restore all that was taken from you so you can get back to what you were created for. You are tired of running from moment to moment. He says that you are ready for long term completion. You will be a mentor for other girls who are tied of wearing shoes that are too big. He says you will show them how to stop running and how to find the perfect fit. He says He loves you.

Josephine

I see you dancing, it's not just a dance, it's a dance for your life. The Lord says you have given yourself over to the things of the world and now you are trying to take back the control you have given up. He says there may be pain but don't give up. He will be there to pick you up when you fall in exhaustion. He says that you will get through this. He has many plans for you. You are concerned for your children. They are safe and you will be united with them. He says to keep dancing with Him and you will reach the other side of the control you gave up. When you get the control back, He wants you to surrender it all to Him. He wants to finish the dance of life with you. He says that because of all you have survived, you will be a great testimony for others who are afraid to start the dance for their lives. You will be a great dance instructor. He says to not give up and trust in Him. He says He loves you.

Judy

The Lord says that a more beautiful person one could ever find. He says you melt His heart; you are such a captivating spirit. You have had your share of struggles and let downs but you are always pulling yourself up. You have discovered a courage within yourself that you have always known was there but you have not fully embraced. You and your courage are now becoming very good friends. He says when you completely embrace your courage; you will be a life changer. You have the gift of compassion and a listening heart. He says that many can listen but not all can listen without judging and with complete understanding. When you listen others will release their hidden secrets and when they release you will love and when you love they will grow and when they grow they will run to Him. He says you are such a beautiful person. He says He loves you.

Justine

The Lord says it is the little things in life that mean the most to you. He says that the big things have always been available and offered, but the little things were hidden and unspoken. He says they have become the jewels in your box. In life, you cherish the little things and have learned the secret to true happiness lies in the unspoken and hidden little things.

Justine, the Lord says that you will be the one others look to for the hidden treasures. You will be able to love and cherish life on a different level because you won't be looking for happiness in the wrong places. He says you will be a teacher to many. You will catch a lot of people off guard because of your beauty; they will offend you by always offering the big things. You will be able to teach *that even the most beautiful gem loves the little things. He says He loves you.*

Kara

The Lord says He sees you! He sees your heart and the hole that lives in it. He says you are not alone even though the pain in each day is a constant reminder of the hole; still you are not alone. Ever since you can remember you have felt rejected, unloved, abandoned, put aside and forgotten. You find yourself looking for things that will hopefully fill the hole that still lives in your heart. You do whatever it takes to feel something instead of the pain.

Kara, the Lord says the hole can never be filled with the things, people or feelings that come from the world. He knows it is hard for you to believe in Him right now and He understands. He wants you know that if you just take one step of faith and give all your pain to Him, He will fill the hole with love, hope, sense of worth and the truth that you need. He says you have many wonderful things about you that are hidden in the hole and He wants to show them to you. He says He is the truth, the light and the way. He will never leave you nor forget you. He says He loves you.

Kathy

The Lord says your heart is so big, you get lost in it. Over the years you have learned what order, balance and boundaries can do for you, your family and your health. You have begun to walk in all that you were created to be. Now that you have security in the heart that used to consume you, you can walk in the fullness of the real you. Your level of compassion and giving is beyond understanding to most. He says that some even try to tell you, or convince you, how to spend and when to give. He says to continue to listen to His voice and follow His steps and you will continue to bless a multitude. He knows that your purpose every day is to be the best that you can be for Him and to do His will. You love the little ones and do not like to see them hurt. You are going to start your own ministry that will be like no other. You will touch the lives of many children and those children will continue to stay to the path He has laid out for them. He says He loves you.

Katrina

The Lord gave me the number five. He says that number is very significant to you; it is how many times you have truly given your heart away. It is how many times you will allow someone to hurt you. He says that is also the number that means grace and you are just that. He says you can't stand to hurt anyone or to see anyone hurt. He says your heart is five times more merciful than most. A lot of people misunderstand you because of your honesty. You treat others the way you want to be treated so you extend honest, merciful grace. This has cost you many friendships because you refuse to be mistreated. He is going to begin placing you in situations where your ability to lovingly be honest and show mercy and grace will allow others to see that true love still exists. He says you will be able to love the lies out of the ones who think no one would or could ever truly love them. You will show them what the love of God looks like. He says He loves you.

Kelly

The Lord says, "What a beautiful testimony you are! The things you have walked through have made you the strong pillar that you are today." He has placed you where you are for a purpose. The teenage girls will look to you for guidance; they will come to you because they know that you have walked through it already. They will see the foot prints of your yesterday and the promise of your today and they will trust you. You will be able to lead them away from the choices of their yesterday so their promise can start today.

Kelly, the Lord says you are perfectly beautiful just the way you are. He will restore all that was taken from you. He says that healing has already begun in your body. Continue to walk in your promise and you will see all that you need in order to help those He sends to you. He is so proud of you. He says that you are priceless. He says He loves you.

Krista

The Lord says you are full of so much joy. You are like a breath of fresh air. He says that you are such a loving person. The Lords says that one day this will be your reality when you are alone as well as when you are with others. He says that only a select few know the real you because you don't allow many into your real world. He says that you have endured much pain and sorrow.

Krista, the Lord wants you to know that you have so much to offer. If you would just lay all your pain and sorrow at His feet, He will carry it for you. You are so strong, and have been that way for a long time, but you don't have to be strong anymore. He will help you walk through all that you are afraid of. When you get to the other side of the pain you will not have to pretend any more. You will become all that you want and were created to be. You will find yourself meeting and running into women and young girls who are going through what you came through and you will be the guiding light for them. He says don't give up. He says He is waiting and He loves you.

Lacy

I see you standing in a large room surrounded by a bunch of people. You are looking around as if you don't know any of them. Then I see you walking alone and you have the same expression on your face. The Lord says that He knows no matter where you are, whether in a crowded room or a lonely street, you feel the same, lost and alone. He says that's because you are. When you were a little girl you walked with Him but you have since gotten off your path. Even though you know everyone in the room you still feel alone because you are different. You stand out. He says you are set apart. You have the ability to draw near to someone's heart quickly, which is your gifting. He says that you feel lost because you've forgotten who your first love was. He says that it is okay. He says He always knew you would come back to Him. He has been waiting and His plans for your life have not changed. You have a very humble heart that loves to encourage others. You will help others get back on their path by sharing your testimony. You will be a light on the path for those who have fallen off of theirs. You will be able to sweetly dust them off and lead them back to their path. He says that you don't look at people for where they have been or where they are; you look at their possibility and show them their potential. He says He loves you and can't wait to talk to you again.

Laura

The Lord says you have known heartache and pain ever since you were a little girl. You have not experienced real love. He says that you have had to struggle every day. He sees you cry when you are alone. You cry alone because you don't want anyone to think you are weak. Being strong yet numb has kept you alive. He knows you think He has left you, and you question if He really exists. He understands and is waiting for you to call out to Him. Lay your burdens down at His feet, He will carry them for you. He wants to give you your heart's desire. He says that all you really want is to feel free. You say, "If I could just have one day that is free, happy and with no worries!" He wants to give that to you. He says it won't be just one day. He wants to give you that every day. You will be free from worries because you will know that He has you in the palm of His hand. Take His hand and finish the walk with Him that you started when you were a little girl. He says He loves you so much and He will wait for you.

Lauren

I see you as a child. You are flying a kite. The wind is blowing it perfectly. You love to watch the kite fly; you love the freedom in it. You love the idea of flying free. You have the biggest smile on your face. The Lord says there was tragedy in your life caused by an accident. You have suffered great loss and, because of that loss you have not smiled in a long time. You have put a chain around your heart and caged all your emotions. He says that you believe that if you never love, you will never feel that pain again.

Lauren, the Lord says that the pain you feel everyday can be taken away. If you unchain your heart and uncage your emotions they will be able to fly free like the kite. The chain and cage are just constant reminders of the pain that put them there. If you set them free, they can heal and in the healing, you will begin to feel again. He knows you are scared. He says He will send people into your life to help you release. You have so much inside you that you have been hiding. There are so many people you want to hug and love on but fear won't let you. With each hug you get closer to the smile you had when you watched the kite fly free. He says that you will love again. You will even get to the point where you will be able to help others remember how to smile and appreciate the freedom of the flying kite. He says He loves you.

Linda

The Lord showed me a vision of you. It was as if you were sky diving and you have the biggest grin on your face. There are five guys with you in a big circle. There is so much love, warmth and beauty in the circle. The Lord says that is your heart. He says the ones in the circle are ones you hold near and dear to your heart. A lot has happened between you and them and there has been some distance, that's why you hang with them in the sky. There, in the sky of your heart, are the memories of once upon a time when the distance didn't exist. You have a lot of regret and they have a lot of unforgiveness. He says that if you give all your pain and regret to Him, and pray for these men, you will see the change from the sky of your heart to the beat of your present. He says that what was your once upon a time can and will be, your ever after. He says your sons will come back to you; continue to pray for them and a break will occur, forgiveness will be offered and hearts will be mended. He says don't give up. He says He loves you.

Lisa

The Lord says that this is a season of promotion. You have spent many hours preparing for the promotion and your willingness to serve has proven your ability to lead. He is taking you to a new level of leadership within ministry. He is going to have you step out in front. You have been in the back long enough, you are now ready. You are going to be able to minister to the lost and wounded prophetically and with wisdom. You will begin to worship prophetically. He loves how you wait on Him so patiently. He says that even with your job, your will be getting a promotion. There will be increase all around you. You are walking in a season of increase and blessing because you have walked so faithfully in the little. He says your children will see the increase and see that following Him

will be the Glory. He is proud of you.
He says that He loves you.

Lorna

The Lord says that you are a true servant. He says nothing brings you more joy than to bring smiles to the faces of everyone you see. You don't look at the world through human eyes; you see the world through spiritual eyes. You are able to see through the flesh, into the goodness of people. You love to speak life into those others see as a lost cause. You are able to pour out refreshing waters on dry deserted flesh and bring back to life the soul of the hopeless. You don't give up on those who want to give up on themselves. He says your tears could fill one hundred buckets.

Lorna, the Lord says He is getting ready to take you to a new level. He is going to increase your territory and you will be able to change a multitude of lives at one time. You have been praying for increase and that increase in coming. You will be speaking corporately to women, teaching them that they are in His will. He says that you will show them how to walk with the faith and confidence that they were created to walk in. He says that you will speak life into them and call forth their gifting. He says thank you for being so faithful. He says He loves you.

Lorraine

The Lord showed me a picture of a ribbon flowing in the sky. He says that's how your life has been. You have just floated, never really attaching to anything or anyone. Just like the ribbon, you have had your ups and downs but through it all you just keep floating. You were able to change with each up and down without attaching to anything or anyone. He says the wind that has kept you floating is getting ready to stop blowing.

Lorraine, the Lord says that you are tired. He says the up and downs are wearing you out; you are ready to come down. You are tired of floating through life alone you are ready to attach. He says that the end of separation has come. The attachments that you long for are waiting for you. The love you long for is ready to embrace you. The completion you desire has it arms open for you to come in. He says that you are ready, you are a brave one. You have walked alone so long; you will be able to cherish all that lies ahead of you. You will be able to help the other lonely ribbon's learn to attach themselves to the ones that are waiting on them. Your courage will help lead and guide you through the rest of your walk through life and He will walk with you. He says He loves you.

Lydia

The strong one! The Lord says you are what strength looks like. He says that you are able to look at any situation and work your way through it. Your motto is "safe and steady". As long as you stay focused, you can accomplish anything, however, in your strength, you do get frustrated. You don't understand why others can't just stay safe and steady. He is going to send others to you that are not safe and steady and you will see that in the difference you make the perfect team. He says in that perfect team you will begin to birth a ministry. Your strength and ability to stay focused will help you be able to guide the weak to the strength they need to stay focused to find the safety they need to be steady. You will be able to help a multitude. He says that you will learn to work for the expansion of the kingdom. He says He loves you.

Madison

I see a bridge over a flowing stream. The Lord says you are that bridge. You have allowed many people to use you to safely get to where they need to be. You have been trampled on just about all of your life and now the bridge is slowly falling apart. You are breaking down from being so tired, at least that's what you think.

Madison, the Lord says that, piece by piece, you are allowing Him to tear the bridge down. He says that the stream is rising. If you completely let go, you will fall into the healing waters that are flowing under you. He says that all this time He has been there. He has been waiting for you to fall into Him so that He can wash all the tracks of yesterday off you, stand you up straight and make you into the women you were created to be. You will walk with others; others will not walk on you. You will be able to help others get where they need to be through prayer and support not through hurt and unkind words. He says that you have endured enough. He says to fall into the water, come into the refreshing stream. He knows that you are tired but you will be renewed, come and let's walk together. He wants to show you how to be all that you were made to be. He says you are a bridge no more, He says that you are the transporter. He says He loves you.

Mary

The Lord says He loves the way you love your family. He loves this because family and love has not always been a great couple for you. He says you have had more than your share of struggles as a child, a wife and mother. You have looked for love and family in many different eyes and promises of forever. You have been disappointed and have felt like a disappointment. Love never came easy for you because trust was never an option and, to be honest it still isn't. He is going to help you rebuild the trust so many have stolen from you. He says your capacity to truly love yourself will be restored. During your restoration you will begin to see your true potential. You have the gift of wisdom. You love to help and talk to people but when they get to close, you push them away. He says that if you give that to Him, He will help you walk through the fear of trusting and slowly you will begin to release some of the burdens that are binding you. You will begin to feel the freedom to help others without condemning yourself. Just take the first step and He will walk the walk with you. He says that He loves you.

Melissa

The Lord says the fear of the unknown, or unseen has robbed you of the possibility of what could be. The words "Greater is He who is in me than he who is in the world" have never really made sense to you. Life has taught you that if you want something you have to just take it. If you want to keep, it then you can never share it.

Melissa, the Lord says the happiness and fulfillment that you are looking for can never be found in the things of the world. He wants you to get to know Him. He is the answer to true fulfillment. He says that in Him is where you will find the real you. In Him is where you will find the piece of your heart that you have been looking for. In Him is where you can find the completion you desire. You have so much to offer the world. If you allow Him to replace the pain and emptiness with compassion and fullness, you will be able to smile the smile of true confidence and love. You will be able to forgive the unforgivable and bitterness will turn into sweetness. He says that He can't wait to talk to you again. He says He loves you.

Michelle

The Lord says that you hold dear to your virtues. You do not sway from what you believe. Many have tried to distract you or confuse you but you remain true to your beliefs. Your walk has not been easy and you have lost a few friends and have had family members turn their backs on you but you still stayed true. In your walk you have helped more than you have lost. He says that you have been a mentor for people that you didn't even know were watching you. Your character has been a bright light shining on those who want to see it and for those who do not even know what it is. Because of your character, those who have turned their backs on you will eventually see that your heart crumbled but you are still standing and in that they will turn back around. He says to never doubt if you are making the right choices. He says you are. He says to keep following His voice so many will follow you to Him.   You are able to turn the character of the ones who once judged you into virtue seekers. He says don't fear you are walking the path He laid for you. He says He loves you.

Oprah

The Lord says that you find yourself asking "Why me?" you already know why. He knew He could trust you. He knew you would never give up. You made Him a promise a long time ago and He knew you would keep it. He knows how much you sacrifice for Him and how much you love and trust Him. He says in all things, you give back to Him, you completely surrender to Him. You take on every task He sets before you. With every move, you make sure He is at the center because you know that, without Him, nothing is possible and you give him your will and plan. He says you allow Him to manage every area of your life, your schedule, your budget, your mind and heart.

Oprah, the Lord says that about five years ago He gave you an assignment and without hesitation you took it on and made it a reality. He is going to expand that assignment. He knows you get tired so He is going to have you raise up leaders and you will be able to send them out to the nations. Through the leaders and your guidance a great change will take place. He says that you have the ability to change circumstances and situations; you have authority in your voice. You will bring hope to the hopeless. You will raise up the children that never thought they would survive. You will offer a chance for a new day to the ones who thought tomorrow would never come. He says the future for many will be bright. He says that abundance will be poured out on the children who will be the ones to stand the tallest. He says from destitute to freedom you will never forget. He says He loves you.

Pamela

I see you as a young lady. You look as if you are going on a long journey due to all the bags you are carrying. You have so many bags that you can barely walk. The Lord says the bags are not for a journey you are going on, they are from the life you have been walking through. You have been carrying luggage with you for a long time. It started out as favors, expectations, secrets, hurts and the bags kept growing and growing. He says that before you knew it, you were carrying bags that didn't even belong to you. You thought you could handle it and that if you could make other's lives easier, you would carry it for them.

Pamela, the Lord says it's time to unpack the bags and give all the burdens to Him. He has a plan for you.

He is going to make your walk much lighter so that you can go much deeper in Him. Your heart's desire is to please Him and He says that you do. You are about to set out on a journey to set others free from the burden of the bags they are carrying. You will be such a great testimony of what victory looks like. He is proud of you and He loves you.

Patricia

The Lord says that you are a confident women. He says this is not something that you believe. You have not been praised or lifted up much in your life. Life has taught you to second guess everything, especially yourself. You are just now getting to know who you are. If you continue to walk with Him, trusting in Him, He will help you find who you are in Him. He says that is all that really matters to you. You have so many wonderful things about you! He says the greatest is your ability to bring beauty into any situation. No matter what you are doing, speaking, giving, encouraging or just being you, you bring beauty. You love the good things in life. You try to bring the good out of others and in that is beauty. He says that the confidence will come, just *continue to seek and trust in Him. He says that He loves you.*

Paula

The Lord says that everyone makes mistakes. He says it is not the mistake that matters, it is the lesson learned by you and the ones affected. He says your life has not always been easy, love was not always available or shown, and for a long time, you were your own encouragement. You have fallen down many times but get back up and have tried again. He says that sometimes you fall so hard it's as if someone pushed you down. In moments like that it takes a while, but you get back up.

Paula, the Lord says if you let Him, He will show you how to teach to others all that your mistakes have taught you. He says that you have a way of captivating others just by your presence; you are a winner of hearts. If you would take the leap of faith, and trust that He won't let you fall, you will be able to encourage others to get up and keep walking. You will be able to show them the lesson in all their mistakes and how to use them for good. He says that He will trust you with the fragile spirits if you will you trust Him. He says He loves you.

Priscilla

I see you sitting at a piano; you are crying and lost in the music. You are not crying for anyone, you are crying because you are so deep in the moment and you are spending time with the Lord. He says you are such a precious gem. He treasures every moment that you spend with Him. You are ready to venture out. He says He wants you to start taking others with you when you get lost in the moment. You will help change the course of many lives when you venture out and no words will need to be spoken. If you just show up, He will play through you and they will come in. He will spend time with them and restore all that is lost and stolen. He says that you, with Him, will lead others to victory. He says that He loves you.

Rebecca

When the Lord gave me your name I felt a fresh, crisp air blowing. He says that is who you are; you are like a breath of fresh air to everyone who meets you. He says that you don't try to be, it just comes naturally to you. Even though life has been a struggle for you from childhood to your twenties, He says you never stopped, you kept going. Never let what happened around you change where you wanted to go and, in that you, remained who you were meant to be. He says there is coming a time when young girls will begin to look up to you. You will be able to teach them how to be a breath of fresh air and you will be a mentor for these girls. He says that you will be their rock until they are able to be on their own. Your ability to mentor them will surprise you because you never thought there was anything special about you, you were just being you. He says that being you is special, you are a true gift and He loves you.

Regina

I see you on your knees praying and crying, your hands are across your chest. The Lord says you keep them there because you are not completely ready to be exposed or to let anyone in. He says that if you keep yourself covered, you get to choose how much goes out or comes in. He says you so desperately want to let go but you just can't. You are afraid of being hurt, rejected and left all alone again. You think that you are okay where you are because it is familiar. He says that you're not okay and the sense of loneliness and being unworthy is consuming you. He is standing in front of you waiting for you to open your arms. He wants to fill you up with His love. He says that you are never alone and you are most worthy. You have so much to offer the world. He says to *trust that He will never leave you. He says He loves you.*

Ruby

The Lord says you are right; one is a lonely number but sometimes one is all you need. Sometimes you get so lonely, and the space around you is so quiet, you can hear your own heartbeat. He says it won't always be so quiet. He is training you in peace and patience; He is going to send you into hospitals to pray for the ones who also are lonely. He says there are many going through their sickness alone. Because you understand the pain of being alone, you will be able to be patient with them and fill their loneliness with compassion and love that only comes from true understanding. When you come back to your quiet, you will be able to rest in peace while you pray for the forgotten. He says you will fill the empty hearts and let them see they are not alone and *they will be remembered. He says He loves you.*

Ruth

The Lord showed me a picture of iron bars and said that you are so strong. He said that you are like iron. Throughout life, no matter what has come your way, you have been able to block it with your strong, iron bars. You have even tried to keep others protected with your strength by hiding them behind your bars but, for some reason, the bars couldn't keep them as strong as they kept you and that seemed to puzzle you.

Ruth, the Lord says He wants to be your strength now. He says that sometimes you get tired of carrying around all that heavy iron. He says that trust does not come easy for you. You love people but only a select few get to come behind the iron bars because once they are behind the bars you are no longer protected. He will protect you. He is sending people into your life to help you learn trust and, in that trust, you will find security and, in that security, you will find true strength. He will be with you every step of the way out from behind the bars. You will remain strong because you remain in Him and that is where your true strength lies. He says that He loves you.

Sage

The Lord says that the world looks at you in judgment. They look at you and think, "How can she be a follower of Jesus?" He says that your body tells your story; you have painted your life story on your skin. He says it tells of the love you lost, the love you hold dear, the pain and forgiveness. Only the ones who take the time to read you really understand you.

Sage, the Lord says not to worry about those who judge you. He will use you to speak to the ones they would never be able to reach. He says you do have a purpose and a plan. He will send you to tell your story to those who will listen to only you. You will be able to speak the language of the ones others consider different. He says what the world can't see is, that through love, we are all the same.   Do not to allow the misunderstood things of the world be a stumbling block for you. Stay focused on Him and you will lead many to Him. Continue to tell your story the way only you can and they will listen and change will happen. He says He loves you.

Sallie

The Lord says that one of your favorite things to say is, "You can only do what you can do". He says that you are right, you have done all you can do, loved all you can love, helped all you help and gave all you can give. You can only do what you know. At times, you feel you have failed due to the way things have turned out. He says that the outcome is not going to change; it is in the process where you shine. During the process you gave all you knew. You are a very misunderstood person with a heart of gold. If people would just look and dig a little deeper they would find the good that you keep hidden inside. Only the ones who put in the time get to find the treasure that lies within your heart.

Sallie, the Lord says that you have so much to give. He knows you are scared to give because you don't want to be rejected. If you would let Him lead you, He would lead you to the ones who will not reject you. You have too much to give to keep it all in. Trust Him, give Him the reins and let Him lead you to all the treasures hidden in your heart. He says He loves you.

Samantha

The Lord says that you are able to seek peace through the truth. You have the ability to bring the reassurance of peace by allowing truth to flow. He says that this is something life has taught you. He says that, in your younger years, you were the quite one, one who thought it better to just keep things to yourself to keep peace. He says that you realized that the only peace you kept is that of the storm no one could see brewing inside of you. He says one day you came across someone who gave the reassurance of peace and you gave the trust you needed to offer the untold truth. In doing that, your life has been forever changed. The Lord says that now you offer the same to others and you are about to be promoted. You will no longer be the reassurance for one. He is going to send you out to teach more of your peace through truth. He will be there waiting to be the keeper of the untold truth and to allow peace to flow in. He says He loves you.

Sandra

The Lord says you are like a butterfly that has found safety inside a cocoon. You have built a wall around you full of all the things you have collected; it is a mix of emotions, let downs, heartbreaks, disappointments, anger and pasted with tears. When you have tried to come out of your cocoon it is very painful so, for many years, you have chosen to stay safe and keep the world at bay.

Sandra, the Lord says that you have one of the biggest and most contagious personalities. He says you can light up the darkest room and that your smile is mesmerizing. He says it is time to stop just performing, it is time to push through the pain and struggles that you must face to come out of the cocoon. He will be there with you to ease the pain and help tear down the structure of you hidden world. He will help you make sense of it all. When you come out you will be the most beautiful and colorful butterfly. He says you have a passion for children and you will be able to help them before they begin to build their hidden world. He says you have a creative side and you will be able to think of ways to touch hearts and speak life into the places thought to be lifeless. He says that you will be able to give hope to the hopeless. He says He loves you and to keep up the good work. He is proud of you.

Sharon

The Lord showed me a vision of you trying to climb a huge pile of rocks but you kept slipping and falling on them. It's like one huge rock, but as you climb bits and pieces fall and you are slipping on the broken pieces.

Sharon, the Lord says that you are, and always have been, trying to climb the huge mountain that is in front of you. He says it is built of childhood hurts, broken family, broken hearts, so many let downs and confused emotions. He says that things just kept coming yet, no matter how many pieces came, you kept climbing. He says that with tears, cuts, bruises, knock downs, failure and start over's the strong desire to, just for once make it to the next day, kept you going. Your heart is so strong. No matter how tired you are, you always have the strength to climb just a little more today. He wants you to know that He is sending you the help you so desperately need. He knows that you have been let down so many times before but He will send ones who won't just take from you. They will be more than happy to take the chisel from you to help break the rock standing in the way of your victorious tomorrow. Once you have conquered that rock you will be able to see the promises you never thought you would be able to have. He wants to be the main one that helps break the rock. He says to take the steps with Him and He will walk the rock with you. He says He is proud of you and He loves you.

Shirley

The Lord says you are like the season; you are forever changing. For a long time the change was in a circle kind of routine. He says it was a circle of emotions; they would change and then come back around. He says the change was constant. He says that over the past five years the change has been different. With each change there is growth, with growth is forgiveness, with forgiveness is healing and with healing is change. You have cut many dead roots that were holding you in the constant circle of the familiar change. You have a new love and appreciation for life and those around you. You love deeply and you have a giving heart. He says that in your change and healing you will begin to give of yourself to those you never thought you would give to. In that giving, you will cause new growth and a new circle of change. You love change and the change you have made in your life will change the lives of many. He says that you didn't think it possible to change but you have allowed yourself to see who you really are. He says that change is good. He says that you are a beautiful circle of love and He loves you.

Sondra

I see a TV that is not on a channel so all you see is the snow effect and no picture. I see you trying to change the channel but still, no picture. The Lord says that this is how your life is going right now, no matter what changes you make; you still have the same result. Your life has no clear picture and you don't know how to change it.

Sondra, the Lord says it's not the picture that's out of focus; it is the glasses you are looking through. You are looking for worldly things to help bring focus to the snowy picture. You grew up in the church but you have run so far away from what you learned that you temporarily forgot what you need to change the channel. There is nothing in this world that can help you focus. He says that if you let Him, He will give you a new pair of glasses and, through them; you will see the changes that need to be made to clear up the picture. You are amazingly strong and wise. Once you figure out and see the solution, He knows you will make the changes. You are going to start a ministry for young girls who need new glasses and you will teach them the right way to see things before their picture becomes too snowy. He says He loves you.

Stephanie

The Lord says that growing up was not always fun but you made the most of it. He says you have always been the responsible one that is an expectation you have put on yourself. He says that yes, you have had your share of self-disappointments but, you never allowed yourself to stay down long. You have been disappointed many times in your life. You have almost allowed yourself to put the expectation on yourself and others to be disappointed or for them to be a disappointment. You have gotten to the point where you think if you believe you will be disappointed then, when it happens, you won't be hurt and if it doesn't, you will be pleasantly surprised. He is going to ask you to not put those expectations on yourself and others. He wants you to get to the point where you allow the failure instead of

186

expecting it. He says you are a natural born teacher. He says that you will get to the point of forgetting all the times life has let you down. You will look at every person as an opportunity to teach. You will be able to reach the ones no one else wants to reach because your level of compassion is deeper than the blood that flows through your veins. You have a boldness that some fear but that boldness will allow you to enter into places that others themselves fear. He says that you have a determination that, combined with your compassion and desire to teach, will help with the disappointments of the world. He says that He is so proud of you. He says to keep your faith and you will succeed at everything. He loves you.

Summer

The Lord says that you are like the mist of rain. He says you are so refreshing. When you walk through the mist of rain it's like little kisses from heaven. He says that is what being around you is like, you are refreshing to those whose life is stagnant. You are a joy to be around. You love to give and serve. You have no idea how beautiful you are, you operate from the heart and you only look at the heart of others. He says you are able to discern spirits which keeps you protected but it also shows you how to pray and serve those you are around. He is going to promote you. You have become very strong in your walk and calling so He is sending you out to call forth the beauty in the ugliest of hearts. He says you are ready. He will be with you and He will keep you protected. He says to stay in the word

and the word will stay within you. He
says He loves you.

Susan

I see a revolving door but it's not the typical revolving door, you don't just go around and around and end up at the same place, with this door you seem to end up someplace different but in order to get there you seem to have to go through the revolving door. The Lord says you try so hard to get ahead. He says you have always sacrificed so much of yourself. He says even though you give all you have it seems that you end up going in circles just to end up some place different. He says the one thing that means the most to you is security. He says this is the one thing that you just can't seem to find, no matter how many different places you go; there is always change.

Susan, the Lord says that He is sending you to your security and all you have to do is give him the revolving door. He says that if you'll come to Him, and trust in Him, He will stop the circles and the change will be permanent. He says your need for security will be no more. He is the key that will lock the revolving door and unlock the door to your security. He says to trust Him. He says He loves you.

Tammy

The Lord says try to count them. He says can you even remember all of their names and their faces. He says the lives you have touched are too many to count. He says that you can't possibly know all their names because you have touched the lives of ones you have never met. He says that you are the ultimate domino player; with one sweet and kind word you cause a ripple effect in the lives of many. Your goodness is so strong that those you've touched can't keep it to themselves. The goodness must be shared and, through the sharing, there is change and it keeps on going. There is no end to the kindness of your heart. He says that sometimes you find yourself on your knees, crying out, just to keep your heart available to give the next day. He says even when your heart gets broken; you still give the *pieces that are available. He says that you are an amazing women and He loves you.*

Taylor

The Lord says, "Hi Taylor". He says, "What a wonderful spirit you have!" He says you have the biggest desire to do His will. He says you have your struggles and sometimes you stumble but He knows you will get up and try again. You sometimes find yourself running so far from obstacles it takes you a while to get back on track. The Lord says that He does not want you to run anymore. He wants you to embrace your strength and desire to do His will and stand firm knowing the obstacles will run from you. You have a strong calling on your life. He is going to send you out to the nations. He says the reason you have not found your perfect fit is because He does not want you to get comfortable anywhere. He will be sending you everywhere. He says this does not mean that you will be alone. It means that you are not to settle for less than greatness because the mate that was created for you will support your calling and be called to the same. He says that you will know him and he will know you. He says to continue preparing yourself today for your call tomorrow. He says He loves you.

Teresa

I see you standing in the middle of a circle made out of the ones you love. They are all holding hands to completely enclose you. The Lord says it is not because of them that you are closed in, it is because of you. He says that you have allowed them to consume you. You love them so much that you continually put your life on hold just to be let down. He says that, no matter how far you must go you will show up. He says that even when you show up, you end up being let down.

Teresa, the Lord says that it is okay to let go. He wants you to start living for Teresa. You have so much love and compassion to give and you give it so freely that you are empty. He says you sometimes stay empty because no one fills you back up. He wants you to take a season of just being still. He wants to you just spend time with Him. He wants to fill you up with living water that will never run dry. He wants you to be so close to Him that you don't move without talking to Him first. He says that it's okay to not show up. He says that, if you show up, He can't. It's His turn to fix them, it's your turn to let Him love on you. He says He loves you.

Tomeka

The Lord says that you are one of the most selfless people. You have given so much of yourself that you don't even have enough left for yourself. You spend so much time making sure others are happy and satisfied that you don't remember if you are happy and satisfied. He says that you don't even really know who you are anymore. You have conformed yourself to the lives of those whom you love, those who need you. He says that this even robbed you of your childhood; this has become your life.

Tomeka, the Lord says it is time to get to know who you are. He says you are a healer and a teacher. He says that you have such a gentle soul. He says you have the gift of healing. You are going to travel and teach those who are stuck in the lives of another reality how to become themselves again. You are a healer of emotions and the mind. He says that your soft spoken tone will make others feel at ease and you will win their heart and be able to share yours. He says, "Together, we will lead them to victory!" He says you are victorious and He is proud of you. He says He loves you.

Tracy

The Lord showed me you standing in the middle of a circle and you were spinning around and around. He says you have become like a stop watch. Your life has become so timed that you have forgotten how to breathe. Your childhood was not easy and a lot of expectations were put on you. You've always had a fear of failure so you've always exceeded the expectations but instead of getting your due reward or gratitude, you got more expectations. He says this has continued and has caused you to always go above and beyond, and now you expect everyone else to do the same. He says that this has cost you much. You have lost many loved ones and friends because of this. He says that achieving excellence is a good thing as long as your motives are pure. What no one has ever told is that you're a natural born leader. You have a very bold personality that can either intimidate or motivate. You are going to begin to move into the motivating part of your boldness. He says a sweetness is going to start flowing from you that you won't like at first but, He says, if you trust Him and just believe He is leading you, you will begin to love the sweetness and as a natural motivating leader, will be able to move the unmovable. You will be able to lead people over their mountain and into their promise land. He says He is proud of you and He can't wait to see you in action. He says He loves you.

Vera

I hear the word restoration. The Lord says He wants to restore you to who you used to be before disaster struck. He says that after the flood, you couldn't find your way back to the path you'd been walking. Decay, despair and disbelief set in and started to grow. He wants you to allow Him to come in and clean up the mess the flood made and help you get back on your path.

Vera, the Lord says that, once the restoration is over, you will be the restorer. He says you have the gift of restoration and that's why so many areas keep falling in on your life. He says that it is just a distraction. You have the ability to hear the heart no matter what words are spoken and in doing that, you allow the heart to be restored. He says that the floods may come but know that you possess the ability to speak healing and restoration over your life and in the lives of others. He will be with you if you trust Him He will give you the words to say. He says He loves you.

Victoria

The Lord says to never forget that you are royalty. You give of yourself daily without expecting anything in return. He says that you do sometimes feel forgotten or left behind but He doesn't want you to feel that way. He says that He wants you to know He sees all of your selfless acts of kindness and all the love you share even when you are exhausted. He says that you are never forgotten and never left behind. He is going to move you into a new role; He wants you to minister to newly married women. You have made it through some really rough days with your husband but you never gave up. He says He wants you to teach them how to be the Proverbs 31 woman; help them keep balance and order. He says this is where you will find your reward and fulfillment. He says that the fruit will be amazing. Family is number two in your life and you will find great joy in your ministry. He is giving you this task because He knows He can trust you and your wisdom. He knows you are led by Him. He says He loves you.

Virginia

I see the statue of the Atlas but instead of a man holding the globe it's you. The Lord says that from a very young age you have felt as if the world was on your shoulders. You've thought that the responsibility of others being productive and responsible was on you. You were always doing more than was yours to do but no matter how much you did; it seemed as if it was never enough. The more you did, the more that was expected. He says that instead of praise you got disappointment.

Virginia, the Lord says He knows that you are tired. He knows the weight you carry is keeping you down so low you spend most of your time trying to figure out how to get ahead or even just caught up. He is sending people that, over time, you will trust and see that they are not there because they want or need something from you. They will be there because He needs you. He says that He is going to remove the world from your shoulders. You will begin to allow others to help relieve you of some of your burdens. He says that you will begin to feel refreshed and renewed. You will be able to get back to doing what you were called to do. He says you are a healer. You speak life and call forth warriors. He says you sometimes get caught up in the process, the healing becomes personal and then you begin to be the carrier. He says that you will no longer be the carrier, you will be the leader. He says your love for people will carry you. Each day you will grow, let go of old patterns and you will feel lighter. Each day you will desire to walk in your calling. He says that you are building a mighty army. He says to stay in the day, walk in the moment

and He is walking with you. He says
He loves you.

Yolanda

The Lord says that even as a little girl you have had a larger than life personality. He says that you could brighten any room and bring a smile to anyone's face. You loved laughing and making people laugh. When you would smile at everyone it was contagious.

The Lord says in your early teenage years someone stole your smile. He says the joy that used to come so easily to you was suddenly hard to find. Your passion for laughing disappeared. All that you loved about life was replaced with rejection, abandonment and loneliness. He knows how lonely you are, and He feels the heaviness that you carry. He sees you on your knees. He is going to replace your mourning with gladness. All that life has stolen from you will be replaced. He says that you will begin to forgive those who've hurt you so badly and for each one you forgive, a new reason to smile will come along. You will smile again! He says that you'll even want to be a comedian. You will make people laugh, and in doing so, you will show them how to love life again. He says that you will be a testimony of what forgiveness will do for the saddest of hearts. He is so glad that you didn't give up. He says that He loves you and can't wait to hear you laugh again.

Prayer

Father God, I seal each one of these letters in your name. I pray that each person who reads this book will be blessed with courage, and hope. I pray that all who you have reached out to will reach back for you. I pray that your words do not become void. I pray that each person's heart will be open to receive all that you have to say. I pray that chains are broken and those in bondage be released. I pray that those who are reading these letters be filled with your spirit. I pray that families are restored. I pray that hearts are healed. I pray for those who need healing in their bodies and minds. I pray that the forgiveness that needs to be offered will be easily given and received. I pray that as each step that is taken another step is laid in front of them. I pray that you will open the correct doors and close the doors that are not from you. I pray that a new song is placed in the heart of the lonely and broken. Father God, I pray for jobs and finances. I pray for restitution and provision. Father, I pray that this is the year of increase and new beginnings. I pray for wisdom and guidance for those who are willing to take this journey to victory with you. In the mighty name of Jesus Christ I pray.

Acknowledgement

I would like to give acknowledgement to the following people for all they have done to support me.

First in all things is God, without Him nothing is possible. I have completely surrendered all to Him. I pray that you continue to use me and send me wherever you need me.

My children Cameron, Nyah and Micah. I love you more than anything in this world.

My brother, Steve Harrell II, You have truly blessed me more than you will ever know. I Love You.

My mom, Jody Harrell, you have sacrificed a lot in your life to help others including me and I am forever grateful. I Love You.

Dr. Deborah Harrell Isom, my aunt, mentor and teacher, you have pushed me farther than I thought possible. Thank you for everything. I Love You.

Liberty Church and Oaks of Righteousness, thank you for awaking my prophetic gift.

your thoughts

your prayer

His answer

Made in the USA
Charleston, SC
03 March 2015